a cappella Carols for Sidewalk Carolers

Compiled and edited by

Robert J. Batastini

GIA Publications, Inc., 7404 So. Mason Ave., Chicago, IL 60638
www.giamusic.com

A Cappella Carols for Sidewalk Carolers is an edition created to fill a number of special needs. Its usefulness extends well beyond caroling out-of-doors, to include caroling at hospitals, retirement and nursing facilities, holiday office parties, family gatherings and even shopping malls. While published Christmas carol collections abound, some are too extensive and consequently too costly for such limited use, and while church hymnals contain all the religious carols, they omit the important handful of secular Christmas songs which are part of the Christmas tradition, and finally, collections often require a piano accompaniment which is generally unavailable to itinerant singers.

So we've created this little volume containing fifteen of the songs most popular with Christmas carolers, all singable unaccompanied—either in unison or harmony—and priced so that multiple copies do not put a huge dent in the budget of the church choir, civic choir, or office party.

Here we come a wassailing!
RJB

ISBN No. 1-57999-093-2

Cover illustration & layout: Yolanda Durán

Contents

Angels We Have Heard on High 4
Deck the Hall with Boughs of Holly. 6
Go Tell It on the Mountain 8
God Rest You Merry, Gentlemen 10
Hark! The Herald Angels Sing 12
Here We Come a Wassailing. 14
Jingle Bells 16
Joy to the World 18
Mary Had a Baby 20
Silent Night 21
O Come, All Ye Faithful/Adeste Fideles 22
O Come, O Come Emmanuel 24
O Little Town of Bethlehem 26
The Twelve Days of Christmas 28
We Wish You a Merry Christmas 30

Angels We Have Heard on High

1. An - gels we have heard on high
2. Shep - herds, why this ju - bi - lee?
3. Come to Beth - le - hem and see
4. See him in a man - ger laid,
Sweet - ly sing - ing o'er the plains,
Why your joy - ous strains pro - long?
Him whose birth the an - gels sing;
Whom the choirs of an - gels praise;
And the moun - tains in re - ply
Say what may the tid - ings be,
Come a - dore, on bend - ed knee,
Mar - y, Jo - seph, lend your aid,
Ech - o back their joy - ous strains.
Which in - spire your heav'n - ly song.
Christ, the Lord, the new - born King.
While our hearts in love we raise.

Glo - - - ri - a
in ex - cel - sis De - o, Glo - -
- ri - a in ex - cel - sis De - o.

Text: *Les anges dans nos campagnes*; French, c. 18th C; tr. from *Crown of Jesus Music*, London, 1862
Tune: French traditional

Deck the Hall with Boughs of Holly

1. Deck the hall with boughs of hol - ly,
2. See the blaz - ing Yule be - fore us,
3. Fast a - way the old year pass - es,
Fa - la - la - la - la, la la la la,
'Tis the sea - son to be jol - ly,
Strike the harp and join the cho - rus,
Hail the new, ye lads and lass - es,
Fa - la - la - la - la, la la la la,

Don we now our gay ap - par - rel,
Fol - low me in mer - ry meas - ure,
Sing we joy - ous all to - geth - er,
Fa - la - la - la, la la la,
Troll the an - cient Yule - tide car - ol
While I tell of Yule - tide treas - ure,
Heed - less of the wind and weath - er,
Fa - la - la - la - la, la la la la.

Text: Traditional Welsh; tr. anonymous
Tune: Old Welsh carol

Go Tell It on the Mountain

Go tell it on the moun - tain, O - ver the hills and
Go tell it, go tell it, go tell it,
ev - 'ry - where; Go tell it on the
go tell it, Go tell it,
moun - tain That Je - sus Christ is born!
go tell it,
1. While shep - herds kept their watch - ing O'er
2. The shep - herds feared and trem - bled When
3. Down in a low - ly man - ger The

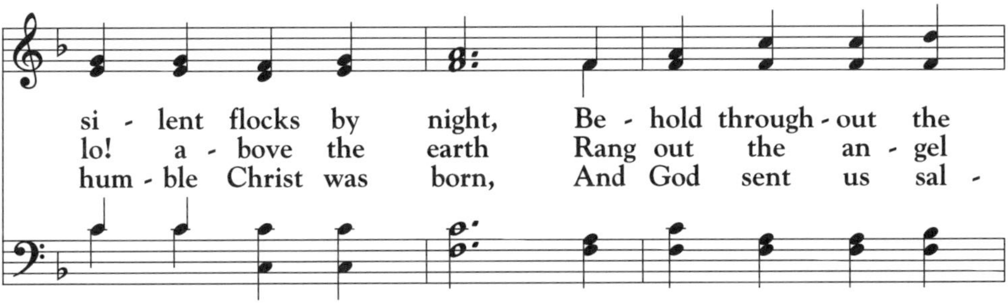
si - lent flocks by night, Be - hold through - out the
lo! a - bove the earth Rang out the an - gel
hum - ble Christ was born, And God sent us sal -

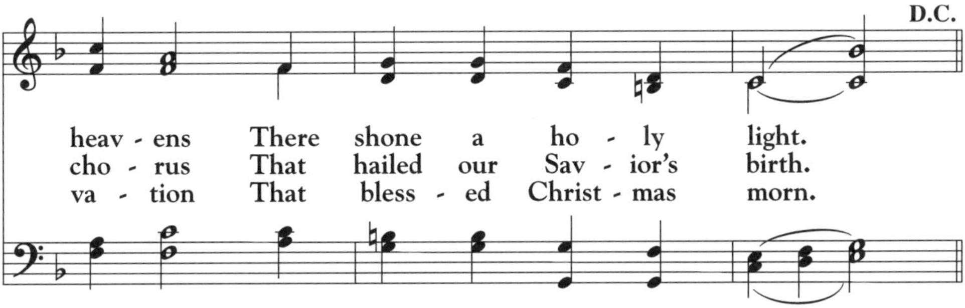
D.C.
heav - ens There shone a ho - ly light.
cho - rus That hailed our Sav - ior's birth.
va - tion That bless - ed Christ - mas morn.

Text: African-American spiritual; adapt. by John W. Work, Jr., © Mrs. John W. Work, III
Tune: African-American spiritual; harm. by Robert J. Batastini, © 1995, 2000, GIA Publications, Inc.

God Rest You Merry, Gentlemen

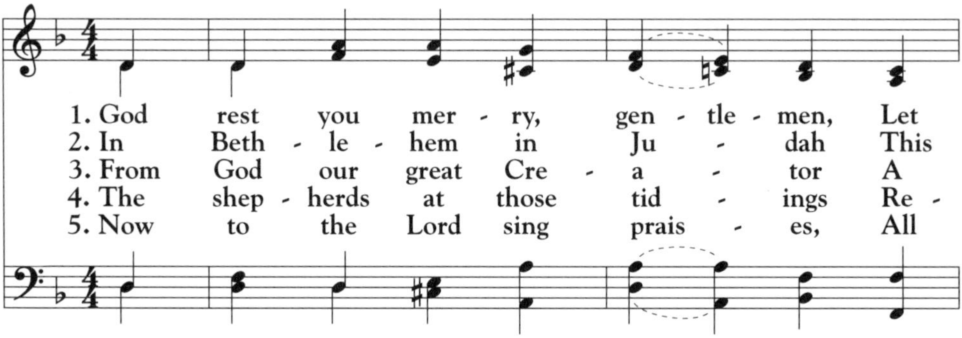
1. God rest you mer - ry, gen - tle - men, Let
2. In Beth - le - hem in Ju - dah This
3. From God our great Cre - a - tor A
4. The shep - herds at those tid - ings Re -
5. Now to the Lord sing prais - es, All

noth - ing you dis - may, For Je - sus Christ our
bless - ed babe was born, And laid with - in a
bless - ed an - gel came, And un - to cer - tain
joic - ed much in mind, And left their flocks a -
you with - in this place, And with true love and

Sav - ior Was born up - on this day,
man - ger Up - on this bless - ed morn:
shep - herds Brought tid - ings of the same,
feed - ing In tem - pest, storm, and wind,
char - i - ty Each oth - er now em - brace;

This carol may be sung as a 2, 3, or 4-part round

To save us all from Sa - tan's pow'r
For which his moth - er Mar - y
How that in Beth - le - hem was born
And went to Beth - le - hem straight - way,
This ho - ly tide of Christ - mas
When we were gone a - stray.
Did noth - ing take in scorn.
The Son of God by name.
The bless - ed babe to find.
All oth - ers shall re - place.
O tid - ings of com - fort and joy, com - fort and
joy; O tid - ings of com - fort and joy!

Text: English carol, 18th C.
Tune: English 18th C.; harm. by Sir John Stainer

Hark! The Herald Angels Sing

1. Hark! the her - ald an - gels sing, "Glo - ry to the
2. Christ, by high - est heav'n a - dored, Christ the ev - er -
3. Hail the heav'n - born Prince of Peace! Hail the Sun of
new - born King; Peace on earth, and mer - cy mild
last - ing Lord: Late in time be - hold him come,
Right-eous - ness! Light and life to all he brings,
God and sin - ners rec - on - ciled!" Joy - ful, all you
Off - spring of the Vir - gin's womb. Veiled in flesh the
Ris'n with heal - ing in his wings. Mild he lays his
na - tions, rise, Join the tri - umph of the skies;
God-head see: Hail the in - car - nate De - i - ty,
glo - ry by, Born that we no more may die,

With the an - gel - ic host pro - claim,
Pleased as man with us to dwell,
Born to raise us from the earth,
"Christ is born in Beth - le - hem!"
Je - sus, our Em - man - u - el.
Born to give us sec - ond birth.
Hark! the her - ald an - gels sing,
"Glo - ry to the new - born King!"

Text: Charles Wesley
Tune: Felix Mendelssohn

Here We Come a Wassailing

1. Here we come a - was - sail - ing. A -
2. We are not dai - ly beg - gars That
3. Good Mas - ter and Mis - tress As
4. God bless the mas - ter of this house, Like -
mong the leaves so green, Here we come a -
beg from door to door, But we are neigh - bors'
you sit by the fire, Pray think of us poor
wise the mis - tress too; And all the lit - tle
wan - d'ring, So fair to be seen.
chil - dren Whom you have seen be - fore.
chil - dren Who wan - der in the mire.
chil - dren That round the ta - ble go.

Love and joy come to you, And to
you your was - sail too, And God bless you, and
send you a hap - py new year, And God
send you a hap - py new year.

Traditional English carol; arr. Sir John Stainer

Jingle Bells

1. Dash-ing through the snow in a one horse o - pen sleigh,
2. Now the ground is white, go it while you're young;
O'er the fields we go, Laugh-ing all the way;
take the girls to - night And sing this sleigh - ing song; Just
Bells on bob - tail ring, Mak - ing spir - its bright; What
get a bob - tail nag, Two for - ty for his speed, then
fun it is to ride and sing a sleigh - ing song to - night! Oh!
hitch him to an o - pen sleigh, and crack! You'll take the lead. Oh!

Jin - gle Bells! Jin - gle Bells! Jin - gle all the way!
1.
Oh, what fun it is to ride in a one-horse o - pen sleigh!
2.
one - horse o - pen sleigh!

Text and Tune: John Pierpont

Joy to the World

1. Joy to the world! the Lord is come: Let earth re - ceive her King; Let ev - 'ry heart pre - pare him room, And
2. Joy to the world! the Sav - ior reigns: Let us, our songs em - ploy; While fields and floods, rocks, hills, and plains Re -
3. He rules the world with truth and grace, And makes the na - tions prove The glo - ries of his right - eous - ness, And

heav'n and na - ture sing, And
peat the sound - ing joy, Re -
won - ders of his love, And
And heav'n and na - ture
Re - peat the sound - ing
And won - ders of his
heav'n and na - ture sing, And
peat the sound - ing joy, Re -
won - ders of his love, and
sing, And heav'n and na - ture
joy, Re - peat the sound - ing
love, And won - ders of his
heav'n, and heav'n and na - ture sing.
peat, re - peat the sound - ing joy.
won - ders, won - ders of his love.
sing, and heav'n and na - ture sing.
joy, re - peat the sound - ing joy.
love, and won - ders of his love.

Text: Psalm 98; Isaac Watts
Tune: arr. from George F. Handel, in T. Hawkes' *Collection of Tunes*, 1833

Mary Had a Baby

Solo
All
1. Mar - y had a ba - by.
2. What did she name him?
Yes, Lord.
Solo
All
Mar - y had a ba - by.
What did she name him?
Yes, my Lord.
Solo
All
Mar - y had a ba - by.
What did she name him?
Yes, Lord. The
peo - ple kept a - com - ing, but the train has gone!

3. Named him baby Jesus.
4. Where did she lay him?
5. Laid him in a manger.

Silent Night, Holy Night

1. Si - lent night, ho - ly night, All is calm,
2. Si - lent night, ho - ly night, Shep - herds quake
3. Si - lent night, ho - ly night, Son of God,
all is bright Round yon Vir - gin Moth - er and Child,
at the sight; Glo - ries stream from heav - en a - far,
love's pure light Ra - diant beams from thy ho - ly face,
Ho - ly In - fant so ten - der and mild, Sleep in heav - en - ly
Heav'n - ly hosts sing al - le - lu - ia; Christ, the Sav - ior, is
With the dawn of re - deem - ing grace, Je - sus, Lord, at thy
peace, Sleep in heav - en - ly peace.
born! Christ, the Sav - ior, is born!
birth, Je - sus, Lord, at thy birth.

Text: *Stille Nacht, heilige Nacht*; Joseph Mohr; tr. John F. Young
Tune: Franz X. Gruber

O Come, All Ye Faithful
Adeste Fideles

1. O come, all ye faith - ful, joy - ful and tri -
2. God of God, Light of
3. Sing, choirs of an - gels, sing in ex - ul -
4. Yea, Lord, we greet thee, born this hap - py
1. Ad - é - ste fi - dé - les, laé - ti, tri - um -
um - phant, O come ye, O come ye to
Light, Lo! He comes forth from the
ta - tion, Sing, all ye cit - i - zens of
morn - ing, Je - sus, to thee be all
phán - tes, Ve - ní - te, ve - ní - te in
Beth - le - hem; Come and be -
Vir - gin's womb. Our ver - y
heav'n a - bove! Glo - ry to
glo - ry giv'n; Word of the
Béth - le - hem. Na - tum vi -

hold him, born the King of an - gels;
God, be - got - ten not cre - a - ted,
God, all glo - ry in the high - est;
Fa - ther, now in flesh ap - pear - ing;
dé - te, Re - gem an - ge - ló - rum.
O come, let us a - dore him, O come, let us a - dore him,
Ve - ní - te a - do - ré - mus, ve - ní - te a - do - ré - mus,
O come, let us a - dore him, Christ, the Lord!
ve - ní - te a - do - ré - mus Dó - mi - num.

Text: *Adeste fideles*; John F. Wade; tr. by Fredrick Oakeley, alt.
Tune: John F. Wade

O Come, O Come, Emmanuel

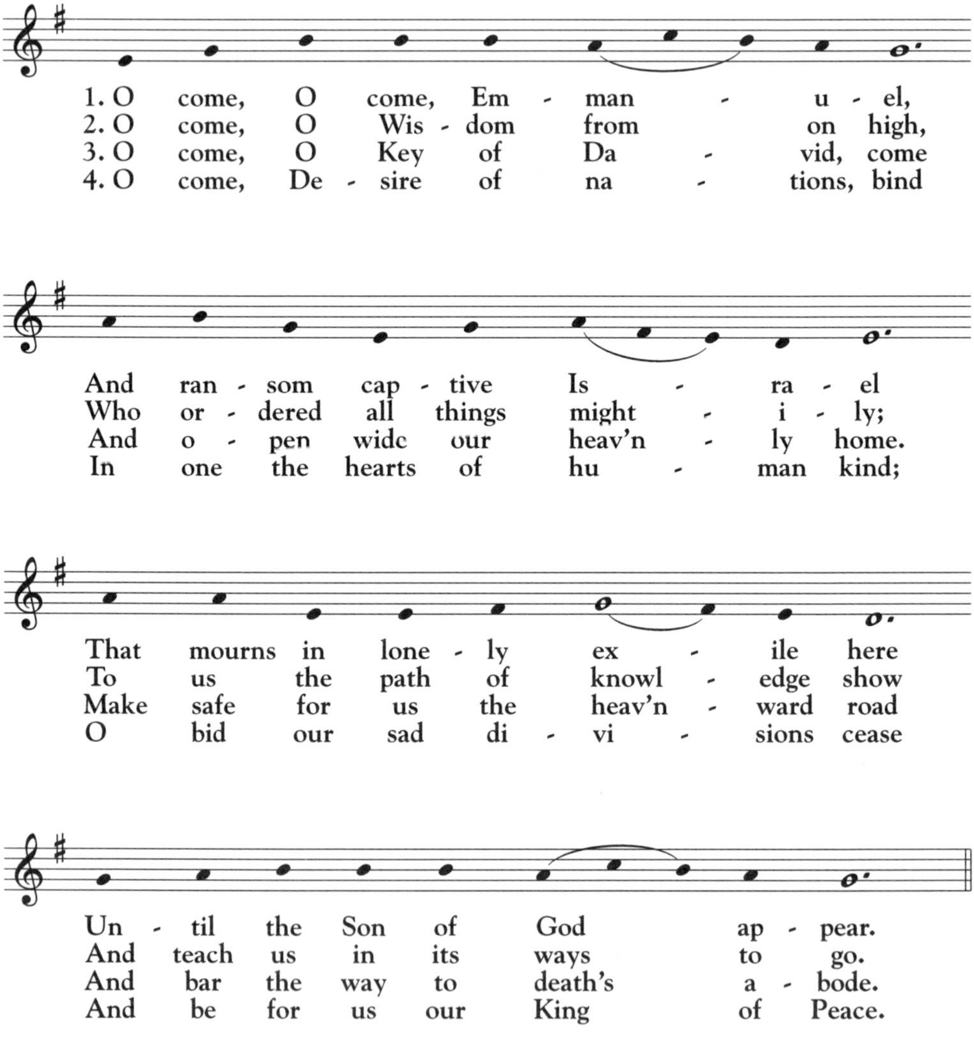
1. O come, O come, Em - man - u - el,
2. O come, O Wis - dom from on high,
3. O come, O Key of Da - vid, come
4. O come, De - sire of na - tions, bind
And ran - som cap - tive Is - ra - el
Who or - dered all things might - i - ly;
And o - pen wide our heav'n - ly home.
In one the hearts of hu - man kind;
That mourns in lone - ly ex - ile here
To us the path of knowl - edge show
Make safe for us the heav'n - ward road
O bid our sad di - vi - sions cease
Un - til the Son of God ap - pear.
And teach us in its ways to go.
And bar the way to death's a - bode.
And be for us our King of Peace.

Re - joice! Re - joice! Em - man - u - el shall
Em - man - u - el
come to you, O Is - ra - el.

Text: *Veni, veni Emmanuel*; Latin 9th C.; tr. by John M. Neale, alt.
Tune: adapt. by Thomas Helmore, arr. by Robert J. Batastini, © 2000 GIA Publications, Inc.

O Little Town of Bethlehem

1. O lit - tle town of Beth - le - hem, How
2. For Christ is born of Mar - y, And
3. How si - lent - ly, how si - lent - ly, The
4. O ho - ly Child of Beth - le - hem! De -
still we see thee lie! A - bove thy deep and
gath - ered all a - bove, While mor - tals sleep, the
won - drous gift is giv'n! So God im - parts to
scend to us we pray; Cast out our sin and
dream - less sleep The si - lent stars go by;
an - gels keep Their watch of won - d'ring love.
hu - man hearts The bless - ings of his heav'n.
en - ter in, Be born in us to - day.

Yet in the dark streets shin - eth The
O morn - ing stars, to - geth - er Pro -
No ear may hear his com - ing, But
We hear the Christ - mas an - gels The
ev - er - last - ing Light; The hopes and fears of
claim the ho - ly birth! And prais - es sing to
in this world of sin, Where meek souls will re -
great glad tid - ings tell; O come to us, a -
all the years Are met in thee to - night.
God the King, And peace to all on earth.
ceive him, still The dear Christ en - ters in.
bide with us, Our Lord Em - man - u - el!

Text: Phillips Brooks
Tune: Lewis H. Redner

The Twelve Days of Christmas

On the first day of Christ - mas my true love sent to me,

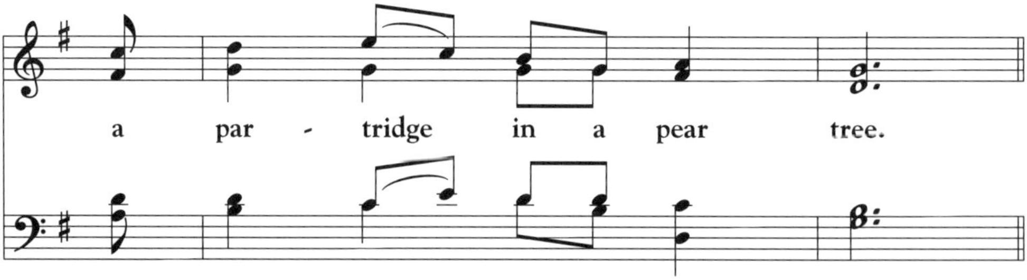
a par - tridge in a pear tree.

*
sec - ond
On the third day of Christ - mas my true love sent to me,
fourth

solos - repeat as required
1. 2.
D.S.
3.
two tur - tle doves
three French hens and a par - tridge in a pear tree. tree.
four call - ing birds

* All verses are begun by everyone singing unison.
Each part marked "solo" should be assigned to a separate singer.

*
On the fifth day of Christ - mas my true love sent to me
five gold rings. four call - ing birds, three French hens,
To next verse
Last time
two tur - tle doves and a par - tridge in a pear tree. tree.
*
All
solos - repeat as required
D.S.
On the sixth... six geese a lay - ing,
seventh... sev'n swans a swim - ming,
eighth... eight maids a milk - ing,
ninth... nine la - dies danc - ing,
ten... ten lords a leap - ing,
eleventh... elev'n pip - ers pip - ing,
twelvth... twelve drum - mers drum - ing,

Traditional English; arr. by Robert J. Batastini,

We Wish You a Merry Christmas

1. We wish you a mer - ry Christ - mas, we wish you a mer - ry Christ - mas, we wish you a mer - ry Christ - mas, and a hap - py New Year!
2. Now bring us some fig - gy pud - ding, now bring us some fig - gy pud - ding, now bring us some fig - gy pud - ding, and bring some out here.
3. For we all like fig - gy pud - ding, for we all like fig - gy pud - ding, for we all like fig - gy pud - ding, so bring some out here.
Good ti - dings to you wher - ev - er you are; good

ti - dings for Christ - mas and a hap - py New Year!

Traditional English; harm. by William Tortolano, © 1999 GIA Publications, Inc.